this planner belongs to:

copyright © 2022 by naci sigler
all rights reserved.

No part of this book may be reproduced in any manner whatsoever without written permission.

First Printing 2022

My Index

Topic	Page(s)

Topic	Page(s)

Topic	Page(s)

Topic	Page(s)

NOTES

NOTES

NOTES

NOTES

NOTES

NOTES

NOTES

NOTES

NOTES

NOTES

NOTES

NOTES

NOTES

NOTES

NOTES

NOTES

NOTES

NOTES

NOTES

NOTES

NOTES

NOTES

NOTES

NOTES

NOTES

NOTES

www.ingramcontent.com/pod-product-compliance
Lightning Source LLC
Chambersburg PA
CBHW050250010526
44107CB00003B/263